Cry Africa The Western Guide on How Not to Fail the Continent

Kayumba David

Published by Kayumba David, 2024.

CRY AFRICA THE WESTERN GUIDE ON HOW NOT TO FAIL THE CONTINENT

First edition. October 16, 2024.

Copyright © 2024 Kayumba David.

ISBN: 979-8227741912

Written by Kayumba David.

Also by Kayumba David

1

Grow a Backbone and Walk out of an Abusive Marriage

Standalone

The Only Crying God in all the Universe
LGBTQ Debunked by Natural Law
The Scandal of Gentleness: Who Was Jesus?
The Day of Reckoning: Leadership, Justice, and Divine
Accountability
The Greatest Woman: Every Man's Desire
The Lake of Truth
God's Interruptions
Faith Challenges Authority
Grace and Justice: The Gospel of Salvation, Social Liberation, and
Christian Pacifism
The Empire of Thieves
Summa Evangelica

Watch for more at www.zcews.org.

I dedicate this book to the countless individuals who have suffered under the weight of these exploitative practices and to those who continue to fight for justice and equity in global affairs. May their voices be heard and their struggles recognized.

How to Fail a Continent
The Western Guide to Supporting Dictators and Looting Resources in Africa

By Kayumba David

The Ultimate Playbook

Title: How to Fail a Continent: The Western Guide to Supporting Dictators and Looting Resources in Africa

Acknowledgements

I would like to express my deepest gratitude to Professor Yunus Lubega Butanaziba, whose insightful lectures unveiled the intricate machinations of international relations. Your wisdom and guidance have been instrumental in shaping my understanding of global politics and the complex dynamics at play. Your passion for justice and equity has inspired me to pursue this work with dedication and purpose.

I also extend my heartfelt thanks to Jesus Christ, whose teachings of the Golden Rule—"Do unto others as you would have them do unto you"—serve as a moral compass in a world where the powerful often choose to ignore this fundamental principle. Your message of love, compassion, and justice continues to inspire and challenge us to strive for a more equitable and humane world.

This book is a testament to the impact of your teachings and guidance. It is my hope that it will contribute to a deeper understanding of the issues at hand and inspire action towards a fairer and more just global society.

Preface

In the annals of international relations and global politics, there exists a well-worn play-book: a set of strategies and tactics honed over decades, if not centuries, designed to maintain control, extract resources, and perpetuate power.

This book, **"How to Fail a Continent: The Western Guide to Supporting Dictators and Looting Resources in Africa,"** is a satirical exposé of that play-book, illuminating the dark realities of exploitation and manipulation that have left an indelible mark on the African continent.

My name is Kay David, and I have spent years studying the intricate and often nefarious mechanisms of global power dynamics. As an author and observer, I have seen first-hand the devastating impacts of these strategies on the lives of millions.

This book is not just a critique but a call to awareness—a challenge to the status-quo and an invitation to reflect on the real-world consequences of policies and practices that prioritize profit over people.

In writing this book, my aim is to strip away the veneer of benevolence that often accompanies Western interventions in Africa. Through rich sarcasm and biting wit, I hope to lay bare the hypocrisy and moral bankruptcy of systems that, while professing to bring development and democracy, have often brought only suffering and strife. Each chapter dissects a component of the playbook, from the selection of puppet dictators to the orchestration of crises, revealing the underlying motives and machinations at play.

It is my hope that readers will engage with this material not only as a satirical critique but as a serious commentary on the urgent need for more just and equitable international relations. The time for change is now, and awareness is the first step toward action.

I dedicate this book to the countless individuals who have suffered under the weight of these exploitative practices and to those who continue to fight for justice and equity in global affairs. May their voices be heard and their struggles recognized.

Thank you for taking the time to read this book. I encourage you to reflect on its messages and consider how each of us can contribute to a more equitable and just world.

Prologue

The Empty Throne: The Illusion of Presidency and the Independence Hoax in Africa

Welcome to the grand pageant of African presidencies, where heads of state don their finest regalia and bask in the illusion of power. This prologue exposes the emptiness of these presidencies and the grand hoax of independence, revealing that real decisions are made far from the pomp and ceremony of presidential palaces. It's a dazzling show, but the strings are pulled from elsewhere.

The Coronation of Powerlessness

African presidential inaugurations are magnificent affairs, full of ceremonial splendor and lofty speeches about sovereignty and progress. The newly crowned leader stands before a nation, hand on heart, promising a new era of prosperity and self-determination. The crowds cheer, the cameras flash, and the world watches.

But behind the scenes, the real script is written elsewhere. International financial institutions, foreign governments, and multinational corporations have already set the stage, whispering instructions and issuing directives that will shape the new president's term. The grandeur of the inauguration is merely the first act in a play where the protagonist wields no real power.

The Independence Illusion

The celebration of independence is a cornerstone of national pride in many African countries. Flags are waved, anthems are sung, and the narrative of liberation from colonial rule is recounted with fervor. But scratch the surface, and the shiny veneer of independence begins to peel away, revealing the underlying dependency.

Former colonial powers and their allies continue to exert influence through economic levers, diplomatic pressure, and military interventions. African leaders are often little more than local managers for global interests, tasked with maintaining order while the real decisions about their countries' futures are made in distant boardrooms and government offices in the West.

The Puppet Masters: International Financial Institutions

Enter the true power brokers: the International Monetary Fund (IMF) and the World Bank. These institutions offer loans and aid packages with a long list of conditions that effectively dictate national policies. Want that much-needed loan to stabilize your economy? Here's a structural adjustment program that slashes public spending, privatizes national assets, and opens your markets to foreign competition.

Presidents may posture and proclaim, but they must dance to the tune played by these financial institutions. Failure to comply means economic isolation and potential political instability. The illusion of power is maintained while sovereignty is traded for financial survival.

Multinational Corporations: The Hidden Government

Multinational corporations are the hidden government of many African nations. These corporate giants extract resources, exploit labor, and influence policy through a combination of economic clout and strategic bribery. They operate with impunity, often dictating terms to supposedly sovereign states.

National leaders, desperate for investment and development, acquiesce to the demands of these corporations. Environmental regulations, labor laws, and tax codes are rewritten to favor corporate interests. In return, the presidents receive praise and promises of progress while their nations are plundered.

Foreign Governments: The Silent Puppeteers

Foreign governments, particularly from the West, play the role of silent puppeteers. They provide military aid, political support, and economic partnerships that come with strings attached. Behind closed doors, they shape national policies, ensuring that their strategic interests are prioritized.

Diplomatic visits and state dinners mask the real nature of these relationships. African leaders may smile for the cameras and toast to friendship, but they know that defiance is not an option. The threat of sanctions, military intervention, or covert operations looms large, ensuring compliance with the agendas set by foreign powers.

The Media Mirage

State-controlled media in many African countries perpetuate the illusion of presidential power and national independence. They broadcast glowing reports of presidential initiatives, development projects, and international diplomacy. The narrative is one of strong, decisive leadership and sovereign decision-making.

However, the reality is that these media outlets are often complicit in maintaining the façade. They ignore or downplay the external influences that shape national policy, presenting a skewed picture that keeps the public in the dark. The mirage of independence is carefully crafted, even as the real decisions are made elsewhere.

The Empty Promises

Every election cycle brings a new wave of promises from presidential candidates. They vow to tackle corruption, boost the economy, and improve living standards. The hopeful rhetoric resonates with a populace desperate for change.

Yet, once in office, these leaders quickly find their hands tied. The real decision-makers—the foreign investors, the international lenders, the geopolitical strategists—set the limits within which they can operate. The promises remain unfulfilled, the cycle of dependency continues, and the illusion of power persists.

Conclusion: The Grand Deception

The presidency in many African countries is an empty throne, a position of ceremonial importance but little real power. The grand hoax of independence masks a reality of ongoing dependency and external control. International financial institutions, multinational corporations, and foreign governments are the true power brokers, pulling the strings behind the scenes.

The grand deception is maintained through pomp, ceremony, and carefully crafted narratives. But for those who look beyond the surface, it's clear that the real decisions are made far from the halls of power in African capitals. It's a brilliantly executed illusion, but one that comes at a high cost for the continent's true sovereignty and development.

This prologue uses sarcasm to critique the superficial nature of political power in many African countries and the ongoing external influences that undermine true independence. It highlights the need for genuine sovereignty and the dismantling of exploitative structures to achieve real progress.

Table of Contents

Chapter 2: The Secret of Endless Loans and Aid

Conclusion: The Grand Finale

INTRODUCTION

THE ULTIMATE PLAYBOOK

Welcome, esteemed reader, to the definitive guide on how Western democracies have perfected the art of propping up useless dictators in Africa. If you've ever wondered how to transform a promising nation into a playground for corruption, chaos, and ceaseless exploitation, you've picked up the right book.

In these pages, you will uncover the well-guarded secrets and time-tested techniques that have been meticulously honed over decades, ensuring that stability and prosperity remain tantalizingly out of reach for countless African countries. It's a tried-and-true formula for success—our success, naturally.

The Blueprint of Dysfunction

Our journey begins with finding the perfect puppet. Not just any despot will do; we need someone with the right mix of charisma and incompetence. This person should inspire just enough hope to pacify the masses while being utterly incapable of enacting meaningful change. It's an art, really, selecting someone who can smile for the cameras while their citizens suffer in silence.

Next, we delve into the murky world of financial manipulation. Here, you'll learn how to flood a country with loans and aid packages, all under the noble guise of "assistance." But, of course, the real trick is ensuring that this money ends up in the Swiss bank accounts of our chosen dictator. Infrastructure, healthcare, education—who needs those when we can have a well-stocked off-shore account?

Turning a Blind Eye with Panache

When it comes to human rights abuses, the key is maintaining a delicate balance of public outrage and private indifference. Publicly, we must express our deepest concerns and sternly worded condemnations. Privately, it's business as usual. After all, why let a few imprisoned journalists and disappeared activists get in the way of a profitable relationship?

Elections are another master-stroke in this playbook. We'll show you how to stage the perfect electoral farce—one that appears free and fair on the surface but is rigged to the core. With a little help from international observers and some creative ballot counting, our puppet stays in power, legitimized by the hollow applause of the global community.

The Exploitation Extravaganza

And let's not forget the pièce de résistance: resource looting. We'll guide you through the art of privatizing public assets and negotiating deals that make Western corporations and corrupt officials exceedingly wealthy. The local populace? They get to marvel at the efficiency with which their natural resources are extracted and exported. It's a win-win—assuming, of course, you're not one of the locals.

Managing Crises for Maximum Profit

No playbook would be complete without a chapter on crisis management. When famine, civil war, or disease inevitably strike, it's crucial to swoop in as the benevolent savior. Send in the humanitarian aid (with plenty of strings attached) and use the media to showcase your magnanimity. This not only distracts from the underlying causes of the crisis but also reinforces your control over the region.

The Long Game of Perpetual Power

Finally, we'll teach you the strategies for ensuring your puppet's indefinite rule. Manipulate constitutions, suppress dissent, and maintain a robust military presence. And if all else fails, a well-timed coup (sponsored by yours truly) can always replace one inept leader with another. Continuity is key in this game of thrones.

Conclusion: Mission Accomplished

By following these meticulously crafted steps, you'll have successfully destabilized a country, enriched yourself and your allies, and kept an entire continent under the thumb of Western interests. It's not about the people; it's about maintaining control and maximizing profits. So, here's to another century of Western democracy in action!

CHAPTER 1

FIND YOUR PERFECT PUPPET

Before you can ruin a country, you need the right figurehead. Selecting the perfect puppet is a delicate process, blending art with science, intuition with strategy. This figurehead will be the face of your grand scheme, the linchpin in the operation to destabilize a nation while maintaining the appearance of legitimacy. Here's your guide to identifying and grooming the ideal candidate.

Step 1: Unearth a Shady Past

The first quality to seek in your puppet is a dubious past. This isn't just about a few minor infractions; your candidate should have a veritable smorgasbord of skeletons in their closet. Look for individuals with histories of embezzlement, human rights abuses, or shady dealings with unsavory characters. This colorful background is essential for leverage. After all, nothing says "loyalty" like the constant threat of exposure.

Consider a figure who has been involved in controversial activities but has managed to avoid significant consequences. Their ability to navigate scandal shows a talent for survival, which is crucial for maintaining their role as your puppet. This past also makes them more pliable, as they will always know that their darkest secrets are just one leak away from public scrutiny.

Step 2: The Allure of Grandiose Titles

Your puppet must have a penchant for grandiose titles and a love for pomp and circumstance. They should revel in bestowing upon themselves lofty titles like "Supreme Leader," "Father of the Nation," or "Defender of the Faith." These titles serve a dual purpose: they inflate the puppet's ego, making them feel indispensable, and they distract the public from the puppet's actual incompetence.

Grand titles create an aura of authority and invincibility, which is crucial for maintaining control over the population. They provide a veneer of legitimacy, masking the puppet's true nature and intentions. The more extravagant the title, the more the masses will be dazzled and less likely to question the puppet's actions.

Step 3: Thirst for Power

An unquenchable thirst for power is non-negotiable. Your puppet should be someone who craves control and will do anything to attain and maintain it. This drive makes them inherently ambitious and ruthless, qualities that align perfectly with your goals. They should be willing to suppress dissent, manipulate elections, and use any means necessary to stay in power.

This insatiable desire for power ensures that your puppet remains motivated and compliant. Their ambition makes them dependent on your support and resources, creating a symbiotic relationship where both parties benefit from the puppet's continued dominance. This thirst for power also means they are likely to take drastic measures to eliminate any threats, ensuring the stability of their rule.

Step 4: Charisma with Limits

Charisma is key, but it must be carefully balanced. Your puppet needs to be charismatic enough to convince the masses that they're the "savior" of the nation. They should be able to deliver rousing speeches, make grand promises, and present themselves as a beacon of hope. However, it's crucial that this charisma doesn't translate into actual competence. They should inspire hope without ever fulfilling it, keeping the populace perpetually waiting for the improvements that never come.

Charisma without competence is the perfect recipe for maintaining a controlled state of disillusionment among the populace. The people remain hopeful yet frustrated, creating a cycle of dependency on the puppet's promises and your support. This ensures that the puppet remains in power, while the country remains in a state of perpetual underdevelopment and instability.

Step 5: The Illusion of Reform

Your ideal puppet should be adept at creating the illusion of reform. They should make grand announcements about anti-corruption campaigns, economic revitalization plans, and social welfare programs. However, these initiatives should be nothing more than window dressing—designed to placate the public and international observers while the underlying corruption and mismanagement continue unabated.

This illusion of reform keeps the public hopeful and the international community appeased. It provides a smokescreen for the puppet's true activities and ensures that any criticism is met with claims of ongoing "progress." This strategy maintains the puppet's image as a reformer while allowing the status quo of exploitation and corruption to persist.

Step 6: The Inner Circle of Cronies

No puppet ruler is complete without a loyal inner circle of cronies. These trusted advisors and officials should be just as corrupt and power-hungry as the leader themselves. This inner circle ensures that the puppet remains insulated from genuine reformers and dissenting voices. It's a beautiful symphony of corruption and incompetence, with each member playing their part to maintain the status quo.

The inner circle acts as an echo chamber, reinforcing the puppet's decisions and shielding them from external pressures. This network of cronies also facilitates the distribution of resources and favors, ensuring that loyalty is rewarded and dissent is punished. This structure creates a self-sustaining system of corruption that is difficult to dismantle.

Step 7: The Robust PR Machine

Finally, a robust PR machine is essential. Your puppet's image must be meticulously crafted and maintained. Hire the best public relations firms to manage their international image, ensuring that any criticism is swiftly countered with positive spin. Use media outlets to disseminate propaganda that portrays the puppet as a benevolent and visionary leader. This PR machine will be the linchpin in maintaining the facade of legitimacy and competence.

The PR machine ensures that the puppet remains a sympathetic and respected figure on the global stage. It shapes public perception, turning any negative events into opportunities to showcase the puppet's resilience and leadership. This manipulation of media and public opinion is crucial for maintaining the puppet's power and your influence.

Conclusion

Finding the perfect puppet is both an art and a science. It requires a keen eye for character flaws, an understanding of human psychology, and a ruthless approach to manipulation. By selecting a leader with a dubious past, a taste for grandiosity, an insatiable hunger for power, and just enough charisma to fool the masses, you will have laid the foundation for a brilliantly executed plan to ruin a country. Remember, the goal is not to improve the nation but to keep it firmly under your control while maximizing your profits. Now, with your puppet in place, you are ready to move on to the next step in the ultimate playbook of exploitation and destabilization.

This book is a satirical take on a serious issue. The real-life impact of Western interference in African politics has been devastating, leading to prolonged suffering for millions. It's crucial to engage with these topics thoughtfully and work towards more just and equitable international relations.

CHAPTER 2

THE SECRET OF ENDLESS LOANS AND AID

Ah, the art of flooding a country with loans and aid packages—truly a masterpiece in the grand orchestration of controlled chaos. This chapter reveals the clandestine techniques for deploying financial aid not to alleviate poverty or spur development, but to ensure that every cent flows straight into the dictator's offshore accounts. Because who cares about starving populations or crumbling infrastructure when there's a Swiss chalet to be furnished?

Step 1: The Benevolent Benefactor Facade

The first step is to position yourself as the benevolent benefactor. Announce grandiose aid packages and loans with much fanfare. Be sure to highlight your unwavering commitment to uplifting the downtrodden and fostering economic growth. Press releases, ribbon-cutting ceremonies, and photo ops with grateful children are essential. This creates the perfect smokescreen for the real objective: enriching your puppet and, by extension, yourself.

Step 2: The Paperwork Labyrinth

Create a labyrinth of paperwork and bureaucratic hurdles to ensure that the aid process is as convoluted as possible. This complexity serves two purposes: it overwhelms any genuine efforts to track the money, and it provides ample opportunities for funds to be siphoned off at every turn. Require endless feasibility studies, impact assessments, and progress reports—all of which are designed to be as opaque and unintelligible as possible.

Step 3: Strategic Allocation

Strategically allocate the funds in a way that guarantees minimal impact on actual development. Prioritize projects that are high in visibility but low in actual utility. Think luxury conference centers in the capital city, state-of-the-art stadiums that will barely be used, and lavish government buildings. These projects not only funnel money into the hands of your puppet's cronies but also provide excellent PR opportunities to showcase "progress."

Step 4: Direct Deposits to Swiss Accounts

Here's where the real magic happens. Establish a series of shell companies and intermediary banks to launder the funds. The aid money should take a circuitous route, passing through various hands before ultimately landing in the Swiss bank accounts of your chosen dictator. To the outside world, it looks like the money is being used for development projects, but in reality, it's just a sophisticated game of financial musical chairs.

Step 5: Ignore Collateral Damage

Now, a truly masterful player in this game knows that the suffering of the local population is merely collateral damage. Starving children, dilapidated hospitals, and crumbling infrastructure are unfortunate side effects, but they are easily ignored when the true goal is financial gain. Make token gestures of concern when necessary—a small food shipment here, a new clinic there—but ensure these are mere drops in the ocean of need.

Step 6: The Token NGO

To further legitimize your scheme, partner with a token NGO or two. These organizations will serve as the public face of your "humanitarian efforts." Select NGOs that are more interested in photo opportunities than actual impact. Their glowing reports and feel-good success stories will be invaluable in masking the true nature of your financial machinations.

Step 7: Media Manipulation

Control the narrative through savvy media manipulation. Use friendly journalists and media outlets to spin tales of progress and development. Highlight the dictator's supposed dedication to his people and the transformative impact of your aid. Any dissenting voices should be swiftly discredited as unpatriotic or misinformed. This relentless positivity will drown out the grim reality on the ground.

Step 8: The Endless Cycle

The beauty of this system is its self-perpetuating nature. The dictator's mismanagement and corruption ensure that the country remains in a constant state of need, thus justifying the continued influx of loans and aid. Each new package provides fresh opportunities for enrichment, both for the dictator and for you. It's an endless cycle of dependency and exploitation, neatly wrapped in the guise of altruism.

Conclusion

By mastering the art of endless loans and aid, you ensure a steady flow of wealth into the pockets of your puppet and yourself. The country remains trapped in a cycle of poverty and dependence, while you bask in the glow of your supposed generosity. It's a win-win situation—as long as you're on the winning side. So flood those countries with cash, but remember: it's not about development, it's about control and profit.

This book is a satirical take on a serious issue. The real-life impact of Western interference in African politics has been devastating, leading to prolonged suffering for millions. It's crucial to engage with these topics thoughtfully and work towards more just and equitable international relations.

CHAPTER 3

IGNORE HUMAN RIGHTS ABUSES – WITH STYLE!

Ah, the delicate dance of turning a blind eye to human rights abuses—one of the most refined skills in our playbook. When your puppet dictator starts cracking down on opposition, jailing journalists, and "disappearing" activists, it's crucial to manage the optics with finesse. This chapter will teach you how to publicly condemn such actions with the right amount of indignation while privately assuring your puppet that it's business as usual. Because, let's be honest, who needs human rights when there are profits to be made?

Step 1: Master the Art of the Stern Statement

When reports of your puppet's human rights abuses start trickling in, it's time to roll out the stern public statement. This is your chance to showcase your commitment to democracy and human rights without actually doing anything about it. Use phrases like "deeply concerned," "urge immediate reforms," and "monitoring the situation closely." These statements should be strong enough to placate critics but vague enough to avoid any real commitment to action.

For example: "We are deeply concerned about the recent reports of political repression in [Country]. We urge the government to respect democratic principles and ensure the protection of human rights. We will continue to monitor the situation closely."

This carefully crafted rhetoric serves multiple purposes: it appeases the international community, calms domestic dissent, and most importantly, keeps the profit machine running smoothly.

Step 2: The Diplomatic Dance

Behind closed doors, it's a different story. Engage in the diplomatic dance with your puppet, reassuring them that despite the public statements, your support remains unwavering. Emphasize the importance of stability (read: their continued rule) for ongoing business interests. This dual approach ensures that your puppet remains loyal and emboldened to continue their crackdown, all while maintaining your public image as a champion of human rights.

Private messages might sound something like this: "While we had to make a public statement, please understand it's just for appearances. Our support for your leadership is steadfast, and we appreciate the tough decisions you have to make to maintain order and stability."

Step 3: Selective Outrage

Selective outrage is an indispensable tool. Express outrage over human rights abuses in countries where you have little to no economic interest. This selective approach maintains the illusion of a principled stand on human rights while ensuring that your lucrative relationships remain untouched. It's a brilliant strategy to divert attention from your own complicity.

For instance, you can vehemently condemn abuses in far-flung regions with no strategic value while turning a blind eye to atrocities in resource-rich territories under your puppet's control. This selective condemnation fools the global audience into believing in your moral high ground without jeopardizing your financial interests.

Step 4: Leverage International Organizations

Leverage international organizations to manage the fallout. Ensure that investigations and sanctions are either watered down or indefinitely delayed. Use your influence in these organizations to shield your puppet from any real consequences. This not only protects your interests but also reinforces your puppet's dependence on your support.

Engage in backdoor diplomacy to weaken resolutions and deflect attention. Offer vague promises of reform and cooperation, which can be endlessly negotiated but never implemented. This creates a façade of accountability while ensuring that nothing substantive ever changes.

Step 5: The Token Sanction

Occasionally, you might need to impose a token sanction to maintain credibility. These sanctions should be symbolic rather than impactful—targeting low-level officials or imposing minor restrictions that do not affect the core of your business interests. The goal is to appear tough on human rights while ensuring that the flow of resources and profits remains uninterrupted.

Announce these sanctions with much fanfare, emphasizing your commitment to justice and accountability. Meanwhile, reassure your puppet that these measures are purely for show and will have minimal impact on their rule.

Step 6: Media Manipulation

Control the narrative through strategic media manipulation. Ensure that any coverage of human rights abuses is balanced with stories highlighting your puppet's "achievements" and "reforms." Use friendly journalists and media outlets to downplay atrocities and focus on positive developments, no matter how insignificant. This creates a perception of progress and distracts from the grim reality.

Arrange for human interest stories that showcase supposed improvements in living conditions, educational initiatives, or healthcare advancements. These stories serve to humanize your puppet and create a counter-narrative that diverts attention from their abuses.

Step 7: The Charity Facade

Set up charitable foundations and humanitarian initiatives that operate under your control. These organizations can provide just enough aid to give the impression of genuine concern for the population's welfare. Use these charities to stage photo ops and public relations campaigns that reinforce your image as a benevolent force, while the real goal remains profit maximization.

These charity initiatives should focus on highly visible but low-impact projects—like building a few schools or clinics in the capital—while ignoring the broader systemic issues. This selective aid serves as a smokescreen, masking the exploitation and corruption at the heart of your operations.

Conclusion

Ignoring human rights abuses with style is an essential skill in the art of propping up dictators and looting resources. By mastering the delicate balance of public condemnation and private reassurance, you can maintain the facade of moral integrity while ensuring that your interests remain protected. Remember, it's all about the profits, and human rights are just an inconvenient distraction in the grand scheme of exploitation.

This book is a satirical take on a serious issue. The real-life impact of Western interference in African politics has been devastating, leading to prolonged suffering for millions. It's crucial to engage with these topics thoughtfully and work towards more just and equitable international relations.

CHAPTER 4

THE ELECTION CIRCUS

Ah, elections—the quintessential hallmark of democracy. Or so they say. In reality, elections are the perfect tool to legitimize your dictator while maintaining the illusion of democratic processes. This chapter will guide you through the intricate art of staging heavily rigged elections that appear free and fair, ensuring that your puppet remains securely in power while the world applauds your commitment to democracy. It's democracy at its finest!

Step 1: The Pre-Election Spectacle

Begin with a pre-election spectacle to create the illusion of a competitive political environment. Encourage the formation of opposition parties and independent candidates, but ensure that they pose no real threat to your puppet. Allow them to campaign just enough to give the appearance of a vibrant democratic process, but subtly sabotage their efforts through bureaucratic hurdles, limited media access, and strategic intimidation.

Organize rallies, debates, and public forums where your puppet can shine. Use these events to showcase their charisma and promise sweeping reforms that will never materialize. The goal is to create a buzz and excitement around the election, masking the fact that the outcome is already decided.

Step 2: The Voter Roll Magic

Manipulating the voter rolls is a crucial step in ensuring a rigged election. Inflate the voter rolls with fictitious names, deceased individuals, and duplicate entries. Simultaneously, disenfranchise opposition supporters by "accidentally" omitting their names from the list or requiring cumbersome verification processes that deter them from voting.

Conduct last-minute changes to polling station locations, especially in opposition strongholds. This will cause confusion and reduce voter turnout among those who might vote against your puppet. The objective is to create as many obstacles as possible for the opposition while ensuring your supporters have a smooth voting experience.

Step 3: The Ballot Box Ballet

The ballet of the ballot boxes is where the real magic happens. Ensure that ballot boxes are strategically placed and monitored by loyalists. Pre-stuff boxes with votes for your puppet and employ vote-buying tactics where necessary. Use intimidation and violence to discourage opposition voters, particularly in rural areas where such actions are less likely to be reported.

On election day, employ tactics like ballot box switching, multiple voting by loyalists, and outright destruction of opposition ballots. The goal is to secure a decisive victory for your puppet while maintaining the façade of a competitive election.

Step 4: The International Observers' Illusion

Deploy international observers to lend credibility to the election process. Carefully select observers who are either sympathetic to your cause or easily influenced. Provide them with guided tours of polling stations and carefully orchestrated interactions with voters. Ensure they witness just enough "irregularities" to mention in their reports, but not enough to question the overall legitimacy of the election.

Prepare for the observers' final report by drafting lukewarm statements that acknowledge minor issues but ultimately endorse the election results. Phrases like "some irregularities were observed" and "the overall process was largely peaceful" are perfect for maintaining the illusion of a fair election.

Step 5: The Media Manipulation

Control the narrative through strategic media manipulation. Ensure that state-controlled media outlets provide extensive coverage of the election, focusing on high voter turnout and the enthusiastic support for your puppet. Highlight the puppet's promises of reform and development, and downplay any reports of irregularities or violence.

Engage friendly international media to publish favorable stories about the election process. Arrange for interviews with "independent" analysts who can provide glowing endorsements of the election's legitimacy. This media blitz will drown out any dissenting voices and reinforce the perception of a fair and democratic process.

Step 6: The Post-Election Triumph

Once the results are in, stage a grand celebration to cement your puppet's victory. Organize parades, fireworks, and public speeches where the puppet thanks the people for their support and reiterates their commitment to progress and development. Use this opportunity to announce token gestures of reform and unity, further solidifying the puppet's image as a benevolent leader.

Simultaneously, crack down on any post-election protests or dissent. Use the security forces to swiftly and decisively quell any opposition, ensuring that the puppet's victory is uncontested. The goal is to create an atmosphere of triumph and stability, masking the underlying fraud and manipulation.

Step 7: The Continuous Cycle

Elections should be a regular feature in your puppet's reign, each one more polished and sophisticated than the last. This continuous cycle of rigged elections maintains the illusion of democracy while ensuring your puppet remains firmly in control. Each election provides a fresh opportunity to reinforce the puppet's legitimacy and your strategic interests.

Conclusion

By mastering the art of the election circus, you ensure that your puppet dictator remains in power under the guise of democratic legitimacy. Rigged elections, manipulated voter rolls, strategic ballot stuffing, and controlled media narratives all contribute to the perfect illusion of democracy. It's a brilliantly orchestrated charade that keeps the profits flowing and the puppet strings firmly in your hands. Truly, democracy at its finest!

This book is a satirical take on a serious issue. The real-life impact of Western interference in African politics has been devastating, leading to prolonged suffering for millions. It's crucial to engage with these topics thoughtfully and work towards more just and equitable international relations.

CHAPTER 5

THE ART OF PUBLIC RESOURCE LOOTING

Welcome to the pièce de résistance of the Western guide to supporting dictators and looting resources in Africa: the art of public resource looting. This chapter will teach you how to encourage your puppet dictator to privatize public resources and sign lucrative contracts with Western companies. Mining, oil, and timber are all fair game. The wealth generated will, of course, be shared between your puppet and your corporations. The local population? They get to enjoy the view of their natural resources being exploited. Let's dive into the intricacies of this lucrative endeavor.

Step 1: The Privatization Push

Begin by convincing your puppet of the merits of privatization. Frame it as a necessary step towards modernization and economic growth. Use buzzwords like "efficiency," "innovation," and "foreign investment" to make the concept irresistible. Highlight success stories from other countries (preferably fabricated or exaggerated) to drive home the point.

Privatization is a win-win for you and your puppet. It allows you to gain control of valuable resources while your puppet receives a cut of the profits. To the public, it's sold as a step towards progress and development, though the real goal is to divert wealth into the hands of a few.

Step 2: The Lucrative Contracts

Next, facilitate the signing of lucrative contracts with Western companies. These contracts should be heavily skewed in favor of your corporations, with minimal benefits for the host country. Ensure that the terms are opaque and complex, making it difficult for anyone to fully understand the extent of the exploitation.

Deploy top-tier lawyers and negotiators to draft these contracts, embedding clauses that guarantee favorable conditions for your companies, such as tax exemptions, minimal regulatory oversight, and extensive control over resource extraction. The puppet government should be complicit, either through ignorance or direct collusion.

Step 3: The Extraction Bonanza

With the contracts in place, it's time to begin the extraction bonanza. Mining, oil drilling, and timber logging should commence with maximum efficiency and minimal concern for environmental or social impact. The goal is to extract as much wealth as possible in the shortest time, with little regard for sustainable practices.

Hire local workers at minimal wages, ensuring that the bulk of the profits are funneled back to your corporations and the puppet's offshore accounts. The local population should be kept at bay with token gestures like community development projects or small-scale infrastructure improvements that pale in comparison to the wealth being extracted.

Step 4: The Propaganda Machine

To keep the local population complacent, deploy a robust propaganda machine. Use state-controlled media to highlight the supposed benefits of foreign investment and resource extraction. Emphasize the jobs created (however minimal and poorly paid they might be) and the trickle-down effects on the local economy.

Create feel-good stories about corporate social responsibility initiatives, such as building schools or clinics, which are mere drops in the bucket compared to the wealth being siphoned off. The aim is to create a narrative of progress and development, masking the reality of exploitation.

Step 5: The Security Apparatus

To protect the lucrative resource extraction operations, establish a strong security apparatus. This could include private security firms, loyal military units, or paramilitary groups tasked with safeguarding the interests of the companies and the puppet regime. Ensure that any dissent or resistance is swiftly and brutally suppressed.

Label any opposition to the resource extraction as anti-development or anti-progress. Use the security apparatus to intimidate, arrest, or eliminate activists and community leaders who dare to speak out against the exploitation. This ensures a stable and controlled environment for uninterrupted looting.

Step 6: The Offshore Accounts

Facilitate the flow of wealth into offshore accounts belonging to your puppet and their inner circle. Set up complex networks of shell companies and bank accounts in tax havens to launder the profits and obscure the money trail. This ensures that the wealth generated from resource extraction is safely tucked away, out of reach of prying eyes.

Regularly update your puppet on the status of their offshore accounts to keep them motivated and loyal. The promise of immense personal wealth is a powerful incentive for them to continue supporting your agenda and suppressing any opposition.

Step 7: The Environmental Aftermath

Once the resources are depleted or the operation becomes too controversial, pull out and leave the environmental aftermath for the local population to deal with. Toxic waste, deforestation, and polluted water sources are the legacy of your extraction bonanza. But who cares? The profits have already been secured, and the puppet's regime will bear the brunt of any backlash.

To mitigate any international criticism, release carefully crafted statements expressing "deep concern" over the environmental damage and pledging to "support" cleanup efforts, which will never materialize. This maintains the illusion of corporate responsibility while absolving your companies of any real accountability.

Conclusion

By mastering the art of public resource looting, you ensure a steady flow of wealth into the pockets of your puppet and your corporations. The local population remains impoverished and powerless, while the natural riches of their land are shipped overseas. It's a brilliantly executed scheme of exploitation, cloaked in the rhetoric of development and progress. Remember, it's not about the people or the environment—it's about control and profit. Here's to another successful venture in the grand tradition of Western resource extraction!

This book is a satirical take on a serious issue. The real-life impact of Western interference in African politics has been devastating, leading to prolonged suffering for millions. It's crucial to engage with these topics thoughtfully and work towards more just and equitable international relations.

CHAPTER 6

CRISIS MANAGEMENT FOR FUN AND PROFIT

Ah, the beauty of crises. They're inevitable in the intricate dance of destabilization and exploitation, and when they arise—be it famine, civil war, or disease outbreaks—they present the perfect opportunity to step in as the benevolent savior. This chapter will teach you how to manage these crises for fun and profit, sending humanitarian aid (with strings attached, of course) and using the media to highlight your generosity. This not only distracts from your role in causing the crisis but also ensures continued control over the region. Let's explore the art of turning disaster into opportunity.

Step 1: Orchestrate the Crisis

While it may sound Machiavellian, understanding the dynamics that lead to crises can help you subtly nudge them into existence. Encourage policies that destabilize the economy, exacerbate ethnic tensions, or weaken public health infrastructure. This groundwork ensures that when the crisis hits, it does so with maximum impact.

Whether through economic exploitation, political meddling, or social engineering, your actions should contribute to creating an environment ripe for disaster. Once the crisis erupts, your prior involvement will be well-hidden beneath layers of plausible deniability.

Step 2: The Benevolent Savior

As the crisis unfolds, position yourself as the benevolent savior. Announce large-scale humanitarian aid packages and mobilize relief efforts with great fanfare. Ensure that this aid is highly visible—colorful tents, emblazoned logos, and photo ops with grateful recipients. The aim is to create a narrative of compassion and generosity.

Deploy well-publicized missions of mercy, complete with high-profile visits from dignitaries and celebrities. This spectacle distracts from the underlying causes of the crisis and shifts the focus to your "heroic" efforts to alleviate suffering.

Step 3: Strings Attached

Humanitarian aid should always come with strings attached. Ensure that aid distribution is controlled through channels that reinforce your influence. Favor regions loyal to your puppet while marginalizing opposition areas. This selective aid distribution solidifies your puppet's power base and weakens dissenting factions.

Attach economic and political conditions to the aid. Insist on structural adjustments, favorable trade deals, or military cooperation in exchange for continued support. These conditions ensure that the crisis serves as a lever to extract further concessions and deepen your control over the region.

Step 4: The Media Blitz

Launch a media blitz to highlight your generosity and commitment to humanitarian values. Use state-controlled and international media to broadcast heartwarming stories of lives saved and communities rebuilt thanks to your intervention. This media narrative should paint you as a selfless benefactor, glossing over any mention of your role in causing the crisis.

Engage in strategic storytelling, emphasizing the resilience of the affected population and your pivotal role in their recovery. Feature interviews with aid recipients, relief workers, and "independent" analysts who can vouch for the effectiveness and necessity of your aid efforts.

Step 5: Control the Relief Efforts

Take control of the relief efforts to ensure that they serve your strategic interests. Appoint loyalists to key positions within the aid distribution network. These individuals will ensure that aid is directed where it reinforces your puppet's authority and undermines opposition.

Use the relief efforts as a cover for intelligence-gathering and political maneuvering. Embed operatives within aid organizations to gather information on opposition groups and community leaders. This dual-purpose approach turns humanitarian missions into tools of surveillance and control.

Step 6: The Financial Windfall

Crisis management can be a lucrative endeavor. Ensure that contracts for aid delivery, reconstruction, and development are awarded to companies within your sphere of influence. These contracts should be highly profitable, with ample opportunities for kickbacks and corruption.

Leverage the crisis to secure additional loans and grants from international financial institutions. These funds can be funneled into projects that benefit your interests while saddling the host country with debt. The resulting financial dependency further cements your control.

Step 7. The Cycle of Dependency

Crises create a cycle of dependency that can be exploited for long-term gain. As the immediate disaster subsides, transition to development aid and capacity-building initiatives that keep the affected region reliant on your support. This ongoing dependency ensures that your influence remains unchallenged.

Promote initiatives that appear to address the root causes of the crisis but are designed to perpetuate dependence. For example, introduce agricultural programs that rely on imported seeds and technology or health initiatives that depend on foreign expertise and funding. These programs create the illusion of progress while maintaining control.

Conclusion

By mastering the art of crisis management for fun and profit, you can turn inevitable disasters into opportunities for furthering your interests. Through strategic humanitarian aid, media manipulation, and controlled relief efforts, you can portray yourself as a benevolent savior while reinforcing your influence and extracting additional concessions. Remember, in the world of exploitation and control, crises are not just obstacles—they are opportunities for profit and power. Here's to turning disaster into triumph, one crisis at a time.

This book is a satirical take on a serious issue. The real-life impact of Western interference in African politics has been devastating, leading to prolonged suffering for millions. It's crucial to engage with these topics thoughtfully and work towards more just and equitable international relations.

CHAPTER 7

STAYING IN POWER – THE LONG GAME

The final piece in the grand strategy of supporting dictators and looting resources is ensuring that your chosen puppet stays in power indefinitely. The key to a long and profitable partnership is stability—your stability, not the country's. This chapter will guide you through the intricate process of manipulating constitutions, suppressing dissent, and maintaining a strong military presence. And when all else fails, a well-orchestrated coup can replace your old puppet with a new, equally corrupt leader. Here's how to play the long game.

Step 1: Manipulating Constitutions

The foundation of indefinite rule lies in manipulating the constitution to favor your puppet's continued reign. Start by encouraging constitutional amendments that extend term limits or eliminate them altogether. Use a mix of legal gymnastics and parliamentary shenanigans to push these changes through.

Frame these amendments as necessary for stability and progress. Highlight your puppet's "unique" leadership qualities and the "unfinished" nature of their development projects. Invoke nationalistic rhetoric and the threat of chaos without their steady hand to sway public opinion and legislative votes.

Step 2: Rigged Referendums

If outright amendments are too controversial, rigged referendums can achieve the same goal. Organize a national vote on extending your puppet's term, but ensure the process is heavily controlled. Use voter intimidation, ballot stuffing, and misinformation campaigns to secure the desired outcome.

Promote the referendum as a democratic exercise, emphasizing the people's right to choose their leader. In reality, the outcome is predetermined, but the veneer of public approval adds a layer of legitimacy to your puppet's extended rule.

Step 3: Suppressing Dissent

Maintaining power requires a firm grip on any form of dissent. Employ a multi-faceted approach to suppress opposition, combining legal, extralegal, and covert methods. Start by enacting draconian laws that restrict freedom of speech, assembly, and the press. Use these laws to harass and imprison opposition leaders, journalists, and activists.

Complement legal measures with extralegal tactics such as intimidation, violence, and disappearances. Employ loyal security forces and paramilitary groups to carry out these actions, ensuring plausible deniability for your puppet. The goal is to create a climate of fear that discourages any challenge to the regime.

Step 4: Control the Media

Controlling the narrative is crucial for staying in power. Ensure that state-controlled media dominate the information landscape, broadcasting propaganda that glorifies your puppet and demonizes the opposition. Use media to highlight the regime's "achievements" and to distract from corruption and repression.

Suppress independent media through censorship, harassment, and financial pressure. Ensure that any remaining outlets are either co-opted or marginalized, leaving the public with a one-sided view that supports your puppet's continued rule.

Step 5: Strong Military Presence

A strong military presence is the backbone of indefinite rule. Maintain a loyal and well-equipped military that can quickly and effectively quash any threats to your puppet's power. Ensure that top military officials are well-compensated and loyal, providing them with lucrative perks and privileges in exchange for their support.

Use the military to intimidate and suppress both internal and external threats. Deploy troops to quell protests, disrupt opposition activities, and maintain control over restive regions. The military should be seen as both a protector and an enforcer of the regime's interests.

Step 6: The Occasional Coup

Despite your best efforts, there may come a time when your puppet becomes a liability. Whether due to growing unpopularity, scandal, or internal dissent, an occasional coup may be necessary to maintain stability. Orchestrate a coup with your backing to install a new, equally corrupt leader.

The new puppet should be groomed in advance, ensuring they are ready to step in seamlessly. The coup should be swift and decisive, minimizing chaos and maintaining the appearance of continuity. Frame the change as a necessary step for national stability and progress, even as the underlying system of corruption and exploitation remains intact.

Step 7: The Perpetual Cycle

The beauty of this system is its cyclical nature. Each new puppet, each rigged election, and each manipulated constitution perpetuates the cycle of control and exploitation. As long as you maintain a firm grip on the levers of power, the game can continue indefinitely, ensuring a steady flow of resources and profits.

Conclusion

Staying in power is a long game that requires constant vigilance, manipulation, and ruthlessness. By mastering the art of constitutional manipulation, suppressing dissent, controlling the media, maintaining a strong military presence, and orchestrating the occasional coup, you can ensure that your puppet stays in power indefinitely. This guarantees continued control over the region's resources and a steady flow of profits. It's a brilliantly orchestrated system that keeps the wheels of exploitation turning smoothly.

This book is a satirical take on a serious issue. The real-life impact of Western interference in African politics has been devastating, leading to prolonged suffering for millions. It's crucial to engage with these topics thoughtfully and work towards more just and equitable international relations.

CHAPTER 8

MISSION ACCOMPLISHED

Congratulations! If you've followed these steps meticulously, you've successfully destabilized a country, enriched yourself and your allies, and kept the African continent firmly under the thumb of Western interests. You have become a master of manipulation, a virtuoso of exploitation, and a maestro of political puppetry. Your orchestration has ensured that chaos, corruption, and control reign supreme, all under the guise of benevolence and democracy. Let's reflect on the key elements of your triumph and toast to another century of Western democracy in action!

The Puppet Mastery

Your journey began with the careful selection of the perfect puppet—an individual with a dubious past, a thirst for power, and just enough charisma to fool the masses. You've manipulated this figurehead to maintain a facade of legitimacy while ensuring that they remain utterly dependent on your support. The puppet is now firmly in place, doing your bidding and reaping personal rewards, all while keeping the populace in check.

Financial Exploitation

Through the art of endless loans and aid, you've managed to funnel billions into your puppet's coffers (and your own), ensuring that the country remains perpetually indebted and dependent. The infrastructure remains crumbling, and the population continues to suffer, but that's merely collateral damage in the grand scheme of development. The true success lies in the untraceable offshore accounts brimming with ill-gotten gains.

Human Rights Abuses with Style

By mastering the delicate balance of public condemnation and private encouragement, you've allowed your puppet to suppress dissent, jail journalists, and "disappear" activists. The selective outrage and token sanctions have maintained your international image as a defender of democracy while ensuring that any threats to your control are swiftly and efficiently neutralized.

The Election Circus

You've perfected the art of the rigged election, turning it into a dazzling circus that legitimizes your puppet's rule. Through manipulated voter rolls, ballot stuffing, and controlled media narratives, you've created the illusion of democracy while ensuring a predetermined outcome. International observers provide just enough legitimacy to keep the critics at bay, allowing your puppet to rule unchallenged.

Resource Looting

The grand prize in this game of geopolitical chess is the looting of public resources. Mining, oil, and timber have all been privatized and funneled into the hands of Western corporations, with profits shared generously among your inner circle. The local population watches as their natural wealth is siphoned away, but they are powerless to stop it. The propaganda machine ensures that any dissent is drowned in a sea of manufactured progress and development stories.

Crisis Management

When crises inevitably arise, you've stepped in as the benevolent savior, sending humanitarian aid with strings attached and using the media to highlight your generosity. This not only distracts from your role in causing the crises but also reinforces your control over the region. The crises become opportunities for further exploitation and profit, a testament to your strategic genius.

The Long Game

Finally, by manipulating constitutions, suppressing dissent, and maintaining a strong military presence, you've ensured that your puppet stays in power indefinitely. The occasional coup, orchestrated with your backing, keeps the system fresh and your control unchallenged. The perpetual cycle of exploitation and dependency continues, guaranteeing a steady flow of resources and profits for years to come.

Raising a Toast

As you reflect on these achievements, it's time to raise a toast to your success. You've played the long game with skill and finesse, ensuring that Western interests remain paramount and profits continue to flow. Remember, it's not about the people; it's about maintaining control and maximizing profits. Here's to another century of Western democracy in action!

This book is a satirical take on a serious issue. The real-life impact of Western interference in African politics has been devastating, leading to prolonged suffering for millions. It's crucial to engage with these topics thoughtfully and work towards more just and equitable international relations.

A CALL TO ACTION FOR AFRICAN YOUTH

Follow the Example of Kenyan Gen Z in Demanding Clean and Accountable Government

Dear African Youth,

Our continent, rich in history, culture, and resources, stands at a pivotal moment. The power to shape the future of Africa lies in our hands, and it is time for us to rise and demand the change we deserve. The recent actions of Kenyan Gen Z have set a powerful precedent, demonstrating that when young people unite and demand accountability, remarkable progress can be achieved.

The Power of Youth

We are the largest demographic on the continent, brimming with energy, creativity, and an unwavering desire for a better future. We have the tools, the knowledge, and the connectivity to effect real change. Our voices are powerful, and when we come together, we can topple the walls of corruption, inefficiency, and oppression.

Kenyan Gen Z: A Beacon of Hope

Look to the young people of Kenya, who have taken to the streets, social media, and public forums to demand a lean and accountable government. They have refused to accept the status quo of corruption and mismanagement. Their actions have sparked a national conversation about the importance of transparency, integrity, and service to the people. Their courage and determination show us that change is not only possible but within our reach.

Why We Must Act Now

Our future is being shaped today by decisions made by those in power. If we remain silent, we risk perpetuating a cycle of exploitation and underdevelopment. We must act now to ensure that our governments work for us, the people, and not for their personal gain. We must demand:

- **Transparency:** Insist on open and clear governance, where financial transactions and decisions are visible and accountable to the public.
- **Integrity:** Support leaders who demonstrate honesty and moral courage, and hold those who betray public trust accountable.
- **Efficiency:** Advocate for streamlined and effective government services that prioritize the well-being of all citizens over bureaucratic red tape and corruption.

How to Get Involved

1. **Educate Yourself and Others:** Knowledge is power. Learn about your country's political system, current issues, and the ways in which you can make a difference. Share this knowledge with your peers.
2. **Use Your Voice:** Speak out against corruption and inefficiency. Utilize social media platforms, community

meetings, and public forums to make your demands heard.

3. **Engage in the Political Process:** Register to vote, participate in elections, and support candidates who align with your values of transparency and accountability.

4. **Join or Form Advocacy Groups:** Strengthen your efforts by joining forces with others who share your vision. Collective action amplifies our voices and increases our impact.

5. **Hold Leaders Accountable:** Continuously monitor the actions of elected officials and public servants. Demand regular audits, transparency reports, and clear communication from those in power.

The Future We Want

Imagine an Africa where governments are lean, efficient, and truly serve the people. An Africa where our natural resources are managed sustainably and benefit all citizens. An Africa where young people are empowered to lead, innovate, and drive development. This future is within our grasp, but it requires us to act decisively and with purpose.

A Call to Unity

Let us follow the example of Kenyan Gen Z and unite in our demand for clean and accountable governance. Let us be the generation that transforms Africa into a continent of opportunity, equity, and justice. Our destiny is in our hands. Together, we can build a brighter future for ourselves and generations to come.

Rise up, African youth! The time for change is now.

With hope and determination,

This call to action is inspired by the relentless spirit of African youth who are committed to seeing their continent thrive. Let us honor their efforts by continuing the fight for a better, more just Africa.

POLICY RECOMMENDATIONS TO END WESTERN EXPLOITATION OF THE AFRICAN CONTINENT

Promote Transparent Corruption:

Why hide the corruption when you can make it public? Let's have all bribes, kickbacks, and illicit transactions televised. Transparency is key! This way, everyone can see who is getting rich off the backs of the impoverished.

Celebrate Extractive Industries:

Let's throw annual galas celebrating mining companies that decimate environments and displace communities. Award trophies for "Most Rivers Polluted" and "Best Forest Cleared." It's time to recognize their 'contributions' to economic growth!

International Aid with Strings Attached:

Keep the tradition alive by ensuring all international aid comes with more strings than a puppet show. Require that every dollar of aid is spent on overpriced Western consultants and products, ensuring the money never actually leaves the donor country.

Encourage Debt Dependency:

Double down on loaning money for massive, unnecessary infrastructure projects that can never be repaid. This will ensure perpetual debt slavery, allowing for continuous control over national policies and resources. It's a win-win for creditors!

Support Lifelong Dictatorships:

Advocate for constitutional changes to make dictatorships permanent. Stability is important, and who better to provide it than a dictator who's been in power for decades? After all, they've been vetted by Western interests.

Mandate Western Education Only:

Insist that all African education systems exclusively use Western curricula. This will ensure that African children grow up learning more about European history than their own, preparing them to better serve foreign interests.

Globalization at Any Cost:

Promote trade policies that flood African markets with cheap, subsidized Western goods, bankrupting local farmers and businesses. This will create a reliable market for Western products and make sure African economies remain dependent.

Eco-Tourism Over Local Needs:

Prioritize eco-tourism projects that protect Western tourists' views over local communities' access to land and resources. Nothing says 'sustainable development' like displacing villagers for luxury resorts.

Celebrate Neo-Colonialism:

Host international conferences celebrating the achievements of neo-colonialism. Invite CEOs of multinational corporations to share their success stories of resource extraction and tax avoidance. Don't forget the workshops on lobbying and influencing local governments.

Permanent Military Bases:

Push for the establishment of permanent Western military bases across Africa. The guise of security cooperation will help keep local governments in check and ensure quick responses to any 'uncooperative' behavior.

Token Renewable Energy Projects:

Invest in flashy, token renewable energy projects that look great in reports but don't actually provide sustainable energy solutions for local populations. This will maintain the appearance of green investment while avoiding real change.

Exclusive Rights to Water:

Ensure Western companies have exclusive rights to African water resources. Privatize water supplies so that local populations have to pay exorbitant prices for their own natural resources, ensuring profitability for foreign companies.

Cultural Appropriation Festivals:

Organize global cultural festivals that appropriate and commodify African culture. Ensure profits go to international organizers while local artists and communities see minimal benefits.

Healthcare Dependence:

Promote health initiatives that rely heavily on imported Western pharmaceuticals and medical equipment. Discourage the development of local health solutions or traditional medicine practices to keep the dependency intact.

Media Control:

1. Support media conglomerates that control the narrative about Africa globally. Ensure that stories of war, poverty, and disease dominate, overshadowing any narratives of success or resistance against exploitation.

Conclusion

These sarcastic recommendations highlight the absurdity and hypocrisy of ongoing exploitative practices. By pretending to embrace these obviously detrimental policies, we expose the need for genuine, respectful, and equitable partnerships that prioritize the interests and sovereignty of African nations. True change will only come from dismantling these exploitative frameworks and building a future based on mutual respect, fairness, and shared prosperity.

CHAPTER 9

THE GRAND ILLUSION OF WESTERN HUMAN RIGHTS ADVOCACY IN AFRICA

Welcome to the grand stage of Western human rights advocacy in Africa, where lofty declarations and solemn pledges create a mesmerizing illusion of commitment and concern. This chapter unveils the true nature of these human rights gimmicks—a dazzling spectacle designed to distract from the glaring inaction and self-serving interests that lie behind the curtain.

The Drama of Declarations

First, let's talk about the riveting performances in the halls of international organizations. Here, Western diplomats passionately decry the human rights abuses occurring in African nations. With great fervor, they deliver speeches filled with solemn promises to uphold the sanctity of human rights. Their eloquent words are meticulously crafted to evoke a sense of urgency and moral superiority.

However, once the cameras stop rolling and the applause fades, these declarations dissolve into thin air. The carefully worded statements serve their purpose: to project an image of moral leadership without the inconvenience of tangible action. After all, why let the reality of suffering interfere with the carefully curated narrative of benevolence?

The Token Sanctions Spectacle

Next, we move to the spectacle of token sanctions. When faced with undeniable evidence of human rights violations, the West springs into action with the precision of a seasoned illusionist. Token sanctions are imposed on a select few individuals—usually low-ranking officials—while the architects of the abuses continue their reign unscathed.

These sanctions are heralded as firm steps towards justice, yet they are meticulously designed to be inconsequential. They create the illusion of accountability while ensuring that the underlying power structures remain intact. It's a brilliant act of sleight of hand: the appearance of action without the substance.

The Charade of Humanitarian Aid

The Western commitment to human rights is further dramatized through the charade of humanitarian aid. Generous aid packages are announced with much fanfare, accompanied by heartwarming images of aid workers distributing food and supplies. The message is clear: the West is here to save the day.

Yet, beneath this veneer of altruism lies a web of conditions and ulterior motives. Humanitarian aid often comes with strings attached, designed to reinforce economic dependency and political control. The aid itself is frequently mismanaged, with a significant portion diverted to administrative costs and corruption. The actual impact on the ground is minimal, but the illusion of benevolence is masterfully maintained.

The Farce of International Tribunals

When human rights abuses escalate to the point of global outrage, the West turns to the farce of international tribunals. These tribunals are set up to prosecute perpetrators and deliver justice, creating an impressive display of legal and moral rigor.

However, the tribunals often target the small fish while the big players swim free. Justice is selective and slow, mired in bureaucratic red tape and political maneuvering. The trials drag on for years, and the outcomes are frequently inconclusive or inconsequential. The real purpose is served: to placate public outcry while avoiding any real disruption of the status quo.

The Pantomime of Human Rights Reports

Western NGOs and international bodies regularly produce detailed human rights reports, highlighting abuses and recommending actions. These reports are celebrated as critical tools for advocacy and change, showcasing the West's commitment to human rights.

In reality, these reports are often ignored or dismissed by those in power. They generate headlines and fuel debates but seldom lead to meaningful action. The reports serve more as a performance piece, reaffirming the West's role as the moral arbiter without compelling any significant policy shifts or interventions.

The Illusion of Support for Activists

Western governments and organizations frequently express solidarity with African human rights activists, offering moral and sometimes financial support. These gestures are designed to signal a commitment to grassroots movements and local empowerment.

Yet, when activists face persecution, the West's response is tepid at best. Public statements of concern are issued, but concrete support and protection are rarely forthcoming. The activists are left to fend for themselves, their plight overshadowed by more pressing geopolitical interests. The show of support is just that—a show.

Conclusion

The Grand Finale

In the grand theatre of Western human rights advocacy in Africa, the performances are impeccably staged. Declarations, sanctions, aid, tribunals, reports, and gestures of support all contribute to an elaborate illusion of commitment. However, behind the curtain, the reality remains one of inaction, self-interest, and hypocrisy.

The Western human rights gimmicks are a masterclass in creating the appearance of moral leadership while perpetuating a system that prioritizes profit and control over genuine justice and human dignity. It's a brilliant act of deception, but for those living the reality of human rights abuses, it offers little more than false hope and empty promises.

A Future of Boundless Exploitation

The future holds boundless opportunities for those willing to adapt and innovate. With new technologies, global challenges like climate change, and evolving geopolitical landscapes, the strategies of exploitation and control outlined in this book can be refined and perfected. The key to success lies in vigilance, ruthlessness, and a relentless pursuit of profit.

Stay adaptable, stay informed, and above all, stay profitable. The game of exploitation and control is ever-evolving, and those who master its nuances will continue to thrive. Here's to another century of Western dominance and the unending flow of wealth from the African continent.

This book is a satirical take on a serious issue. The real-life impact of Western interference in African politics has been devastating, leading to prolonged suffering for millions. It's crucial to engage with these topics thoughtfully and work towards more just and equitable international relations.

Epilogue

Looking Forward

As we look to the future, the opportunities for exploiting Africa continue to grow, presenting new frontiers for profit and control. With emerging technologies and global challenges such as climate change, there are endless ways to refine and perfect the strategies outlined in this book. The evolving landscape offers fresh avenues to maintain dominance, extract resources, and ensure perpetual dependency. Stay vigilant, stay ruthless, and above all, stay profitable.

Embracing New Technologies

The advent of new technologies opens up vast possibilities for exploitation. From advanced mining techniques to sophisticated surveillance systems, technology can be leveraged to enhance resource extraction and tighten control over populations. Drones, for example, can be used both to survey untapped mineral deposits and to monitor dissenting communities, ensuring that operations remain undisturbed.

Financial technologies, or fintech, offer innovative ways to funnel money and obscure financial trails. Cryptocurrencies and blockchain can be used to create new avenues for laundering profits while maintaining an appearance of transparency and modernity. These technologies enable you to stay ahead of regulatory scrutiny and maximize financial gains.

Climate Change: A Double-Edged Sword

Climate change presents both challenges and opportunities. On one hand, it exacerbates existing vulnerabilities, creating more frequent and severe crises such as droughts, floods, and food shortages. On the other hand, these crises provide perfect pretexts for increased intervention and exploitation. Humanitarian aid, climate adaptation funds, and disaster relief become tools for furthering control and extracting concessions.

Promote and invest in projects under the guise of sustainability and green energy. Solar farms, wind turbines, and biofuel plantations can be developed on vast tracts of land, often displacing local communities and appropriating their land. These projects, while touted as environmentally friendly, serve as yet another method to control valuable resources and generate profits under the banner of corporate social responsibility.

The Digital Divide

The growing digital divide in Africa offers another avenue for exploitation. By controlling access to information and technology, you can shape narratives and stifle dissent. Internet access, social media platforms, and digital infrastructure should be monopolized and monitored. This not only curtails the flow of information that could spark resistance but also provides a treasure trove of data to monitor and manipulate public opinion.

Invest in digital education programs and tech startups that align with your interests. These initiatives can be used to foster dependency on Western technology and expertise, ensuring that the local workforce remains tied to your technological infrastructure and intellectual property. The digital economy, thus, becomes another sphere of influence and control.

Strategic Alliances and Soft Power

As traditional methods of exploitation evolve, so too should your alliances and strategies of soft power. Forge partnerships with local elites, multinational corporations, and international organizations. These alliances provide a veneer of legitimacy and shared interest, masking the underlying exploitation. Use cultural exchanges, development programs, and international forums to project an image of benevolence and cooperation.

Educational programs and scholarships can create a generation of leaders who are ideologically aligned with your interests. By cultivating these relationships early, you ensure a continuous supply of compliant leaders ready to support your agenda. Soft power, wielded effectively, can be just as potent as military might in maintaining control and influence.

Continuous Innovation in Manipulation

The tactics outlined in this book are not static; they must continuously evolve to adapt to changing circumstances. Invest in research and development to stay ahead of potential challenges and threats. Psychological operations, propaganda techniques, and social engineering should be constantly refined to ensure their effectiveness.

Leverage big data and artificial intelligence to predict and preempt resistance movements. By analyzing social media trends, economic indicators, and political sentiments, you can stay several steps ahead of any potential opposition. This proactive approach ensures that your control remains unchallenged and your exploitation uninterrupted.

Don't miss out!

Visit the website below and you can sign up to receive emails whenever Kayumba David publishes a new book. There's no charge and no obligation.

https://books2read.com/r/B-A-KRSOC-APVCF

BOOKS 2 READ

Connecting independent readers to independent writers.

Did you love *Cry Africa The Western Guide on How Not to Fail the Continent*? Then you should read *HARVESTING ILLUSIONS:The Global Greed and the Pan-African Paradox*[1] by Kayumba David!

[2]

In a world where the relentless pursuit of wealth and power has overshadowed the fundamental values of compassion, sustainability, and equity, this book serves as a satirical mirror reflecting our collective absurdities.

Through the lens of sarcasm and irony, we delve into the grand illusion of ownership, the deceptive allure of progress, and the hollow promises of those who hold the reins of power. It is a call

---

1. https://books2read.com/u/3kjn16

2. https://books2read.com/u/3kjn16

to reevaluate our priorities, to shift our focus from exploitation to stewardship, and to embrace a future where the true measure of success is not how much we take, but how much we give back.

This book is dedicated to the less privileged of this world who struggle to live, to those whose daily lives are marked by resilience in the face of systemic inequities. May their struggles inspire us to create a world where justice, equity, and sustainability are not mere ideals, but lived realities.

Read more at www.zcews.org.